DIY Woodworking Projects

Simple Carpentry Projects for Kids

Copyright © 2021

All rights reserved.

DEDICATION

The author and publisher have provided this e-book to you for your personal use only. You may not make this e-book publicly available in any way. Copyright infringement is against the law. If you believe the copy of this e-book you are reading infringes on the author's copyright, please notify the publisher at: https://us.macmillan.com/piracy

Contents

DIY Catapult..1
Homemade Candy Dispenser..........................3
Wood Robot Toy...10
Wooden Planter Box......................................14
Bird Houses..17
Camping Tent...27
Martial Arts Belt Display.............................33
Dress-Up Clothes Storage...........................43

DIY Catapult

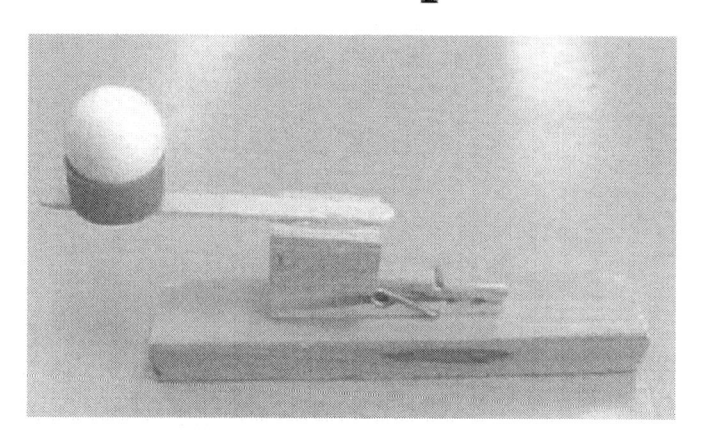

What You'll Need

Wood Block: It needs to be approx 6"x2"x1".

Clothespin With a Spring

1" Wood Cube

Popsicle Stick: You can double up and stick 2 sticks together for extra strength.

Plastic Bottle Cap

Wood Glue

Instructions

1. Take the 6" block and lay it on a flat surface.
2. Glue the clothespin to it, centered lengthwise.
3. When the glue has set, glue the 1" cube to the open end of the clothespin.
4. Glue the Popsicle stick to the cube.
5. Glue the bottle lid to the Popsicle stick, leaving enough space at the tip of the Popsicle stick to push it down with the tip of your finger to fire your catapult.

How to Use Your Catapult

Load your catapult by placing a ping pong ball into the bottle lid.

Move your catapult around to aim at your target.

When ready to fire, hold down the front end of your catapult, pull down the Popsicle stick with the tip of your finger, and release.

Homemade Candy Dispenser

What You'll Need

2″ x 6″ board, 24″ long (The actual size of a 2″ x 6″ board is 1`1/2″ x 5 1/2″.)

Cut the board as follows:

2 1 1/2″ x 5 1/2″ x 5 1/2″ boards (top and base)

DIY Woodworking Projects

2 1 1/2" x 1 3/4" x 5 1/2" boards (sides)

1" x 1 7/8" x 11" board (slide)

Tape measure

Pencil

Pocketknife

Sandpaper

Wood glue

1 dowel or peg about 1/4" in diameter, 4" long

1 dowel or peg about 1/4" in diameter, 2" long

A clean quart or pint canning jar with its metal ring

Crosscut saw for sawing across the grain

Ripsaw for sawing with the grain

Drill

Drill bit, sized for pre-drilling 2 1/2" holes

7/8" spade bit

Countersink bit (so driven screws are flush)

Screwdriver

12 wood screws, 2 1/2" long

4 flat-head brads for nailing jar ring to top of dispenser

Small drill bit for pre-drilling brad holes in jar ring

Jelly beans or gumballs

Instructions

1. Cut all the boards to size and sand smooth.

2. Glue and screw the base onto the sides.

DIY Woodworking Projects

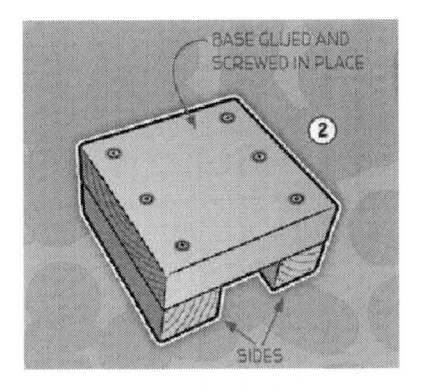

3. Pencil an X from corner to corner on the top board.

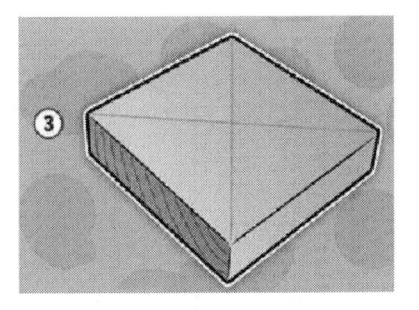

4. Drill a 7/8" hole through the center of the top board.

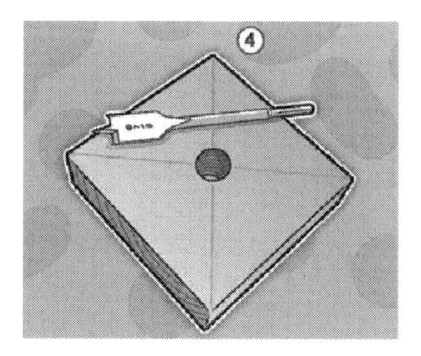

5. Glue and screw the top board onto the sides and base. Sand the slide until it moves smoothly in the square hole in the center of the dispenser.

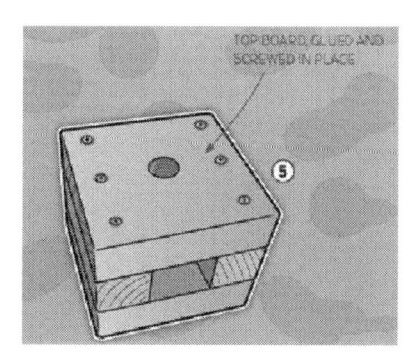

6. Drill a hole 3/4" from the front of the slide. This is for the 4" peg or dowel. Drill a hole 1/2" from the back of the slide. This is for the 2" peg or dowel. Glue the 4" peg or dowel in the front hole on the slide.

DIY Woodworking Projects

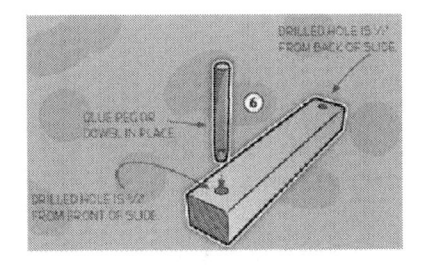

7. Push the slide into place until it stops at the 4" peg. Draw a circle through the 7/8" hole on the top board onto the slide.

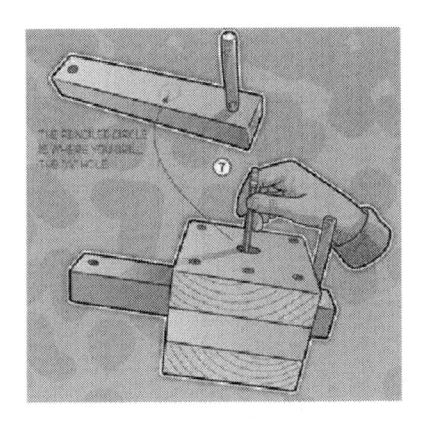

8. Drill a 7/8" hole 3/8" deep into the slide as shown.

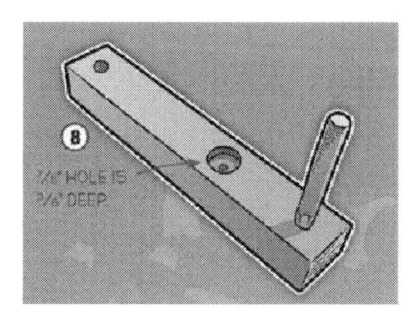

9. Bevel the 7/8″ slide hole with the pocketknife and sand smooth.
10. Drill and nail the jar ring onto the top board.

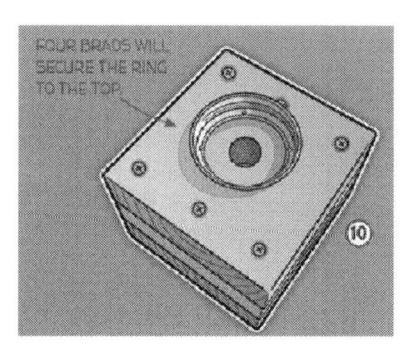

11. Push the slide into place. When the slide is pushed in all the way, the hole in the top and the hole in the slide should line up. Glue the 2" peg or dowel onto the back of the slide.

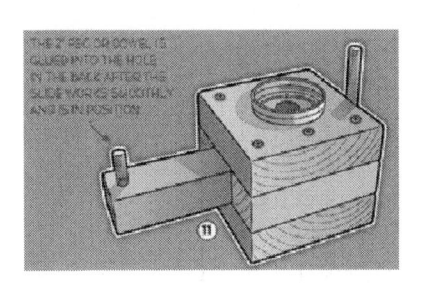

12. Fill the jar with candy, screw it onto the ring and your dispenser is complete.

DIY Woodworking Projects

Wood Robot Toy

What You'll Need

an assortment of wooden blocks and scraps of wood (I used blocks from this and this sets) wood glue and polyurethane glue

drill

heavy-duty string

woodburning pen

Instructions

Toy Robot: Woodworking Process

13. I love using wooden blocks for making new toys. For one thing, you don't need to have a lot of tools to work with wooden blocks: everything comes already pre-cut. In addition to that, I often see wooden blocks in thrift stores, so it's easy to

replenish our supply for new projects and give some new life to old toys. As a result, we have a pretty good collection of blocks of different sizes and grains.

14.   For the robot, we took two cuboids and four cubes. If you don't have wooden blocks, but want to cut them from boards, the dimensions of the cubes were 1.5×1.5×1.5" (like in this set), and the cuboids were 2.5×2.5×1.5" (they came from this Melissa & Doug set). The combination of light and dark wood in one project always looks exciting, so I also used a 1/4" scrap of a cherry board for making a panel on the front of the robot. That little front panel was actually the most complicated part of the whole toy robot project.

Making of the Front Panel

1. Making the front panel of the wood robot toy

2. To make the panel, cut a little 1.25×2" rectangle. Using a ruler and a pencil, mark six buttons on it. With the help of a miniature miter box, make the straight cuts, then widen them with a needle file. Glue the panel to the body block with wood glue and put a weight on it for a while.
3. For stamping "1, 2, 3" and "A, B, C" on the buttons, I got to finally use this stamp set I got last Christmas. I seemed to have so many ideas when I received it, but it's the first project I

used it for! I also considered writing or woodburning the numbers.

4.

Wooden Planter Box

What You'll Need

saw

screwdriver

tape measure

galvanized screws

mounting brackets

boards

Instructions

1. Cut and Assemble Boards

Determine the size of the planter box. It is best to use pressure-treated wood or cedar.

Cut the side and end pieces to the size you want. Then fasten them together using galvanized screws. Measure the box's inside length and width. Cut a piece to fit in the bottom. Secure the bottom through the sides with galvanized screws.

2. Add Cleats and Drill Drainage Holes

Attach cleats to the bottom of the box. This will give you a nice profile and keep the box from damaging the railing over time.

Drill three or four drainage holes in the bottom of the box.

3. Cut and Insert a Liner

Cut a piece of vinyl or nylon screen to fit into the bottom of the box. The screen will help hold gravel and dirt in the box.

Attach to the Deck

You can screw the box directly to your deck railing. Another option is to use a store-bought bracket system that attaches to the side of the railing.

DIY Woodworking Projects

Bird Houses

What You'll Need

3 boards of 6' x 8" cedar fence board (dog eared top is ok)

1 - 1/2" wooden dowel

1 roll 10" aluminum flashing

Snips for cutting metal

wood glue

1" or bigger brad nails/or an Arrow electric brad nailer

table saw (makes it easier for some cuts, but only required for making shingles)

A couple of packages of wooden shims (for shingles if no table saw)

jig saw

2 1/4" hole saw and a drill

Arrow T50 stapler

T50 9/16" Arrow staples

T50 3/8" Arrow staples

Behr paint stain samples (in colors of your choice)

foam brushes

chip brushes

Instructions

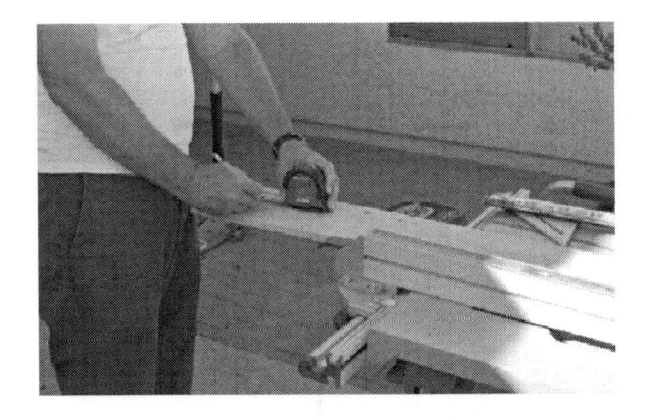

1. FRONT/BACK: Use the provided templates below as a guide. Take one of the fence boards and lay it down flat on a table. Start at the bottom of the board, use a ruler and pencil and sketch out the shape of the front of the bird house on the board.

At the top of the sketch, cut the board straight across so you have a piece that only needs the angles cut out to complete. Take this cut piece and lay it on top of the remaining longer piece.

Clamp or temporarily screw the pieces together so that you can cut out the front and back pieces in one shot. Use the jig saw and follow the lines. You should now have the profile of your bird house cut.

tip: screw two pieces of wood together to get two identical pieces

SIDES: Now cut two simple rectangles to form the sides and connect the front and back pieces. The profile of the bird house will determine the height of the side. The width should be about 4". This width will allow your roof to overhang the sides later.

ROOF: Take a fence board and measure 8" from the end. It generally will look better if you make this cut with an angle on it so you get a nice tight peak. It does not have to be exact. Take your jig saw and set it to about 30 degrees for template 1 and 25 degrees for template 2. Make the cut. Set aside the piece you just cut and return to the left over board. From the cut end with the angle on it, measure 9 1/4". Return the saw back to 0 degrees and make the cut.

DETAIL: Template 2 has a simple cut out affixed to the front for some extra dimension. Just trace out the design on another piece and cut it out with the jig saw. To make the small roof detail on this piece, use the same technique for making the roof. The width on these pieces is only 1". Adjust the length to what you feel looks best. Template 1 has some trim applied. It is approximately 1/2" X 1/4" wide. A table saw was used to make these, but you could use the jig saw to carefully rip a 1/4" (x 24") off the edge of a fence board to end up with 1/4" x 3/4" pieces.

SHINGLES: Optionally you can go the extra mile and cut out approximately 60 shingles.

Option 1- If you don't have a table saw you might consider using a pack of wooden leveling shims and cutting them down.

Option 2- Using the table saw rip three pieces the full length of the board to 1 1/2" wide. Next, take the three pieces you ripped and turn them on their side (the short edge should be down on the table). Adjust the blade so that it is about 1/4" away from the fence. Run the pieces through so that you are splitting them in half. You then have 6 - 1/4" x 1 1/2" strips. Stack then together and start cutting them into 2 1/2" x 1 1/2" "tiles." If you don't have a table saw you might consider using a pack of wooden leveling shims and cutting them down.

DIY Woodworking Projects

2. Assemble birdhouse pieces with wood glue and brad nailer

3. Sand birdhouse smooth

4. Using hole saw, drill hole for opening

5. Using Behr paint stain samples, let kids stain the houses. Use different stains for the trim to allow it to pop.

TIP: To save a little money and play with multiple colors check out the Behr paint stain samples at the Home Depot (this is the only place we've found them so far). You can have them tinted to any Behr paint stain color. And you don't have to pay $15+ for a quart of stain! We do the same thing with small paint samples for other wood craft projects.

DIY Woodworking Projects

6. Gauge the length of the shingles and trim you want to use and cut to size. (shingles and trim are whatever you prefer – our shingles were 1 1/2" x 2 1/2")

7. Using Arrow Fastener stapler, staple shingles to roof of birdhouse

from the bottom up. Use a hammer to assure staples are flush with wood.

8. Paint shingles in a contrasting color stain.

9. Measure and cut aluminum flashing to size to cover peak of houses. Secure with Arrow stapler and hammer into shape.

DIY Woodworking Projects

10. Drill a 1/2" hole under the large hole for dowel perch. Add wood glue to one end of the dowel and put into hole. Once dry and secure, place birdhouses onto platforms and wait for birds!

Camping Tent

What You'll Need

(4) 1 x 2 piece of wood at 42" long ($2.16)

At Lowe's I had them cut down (1) 1 x 2 x 8 which cost $1.08 into my (2) 42" long pieces

(1) 3/4" diameter dowel at 48" long ($2.85)

2.5 total yards of fabric ($2.25/yard x 2.5 = $5.63)

1.5 total yards of ribbon (leftovers)

Drill with a 3/4" drill bit

This tent is really easy to create, and what's even better is that you can put it up and take it down very easily with each use. I made it so it can be easily assembled and just as easy to disassemble for storage. More on that later...

Instructions

1. (2 minutes)

To start off, I drilled a 3/4" hole at each end of the 1 x 2 piece of wood. The Mister and I set up a "drilling station" by creating two piles of stacked wood so the 1 x 2 could bridge across the top. As an alternative, you can drill through your piece of lumber with a scrap piece underneath. Either method will work.

One hole of each piece will be for the peak of the tent, while the other hole will be for the ribbon to tie through. Keep reading and it'll all come together...

2. (1 minute)

Once the holes were drilled, I fed one end of the dowel through two of the 1 x 2's, then fed the other end of the dowel through the other two 1 x 2's.

Note: The drill bit size needs to match the dowel size, so it fits snug. I used a 3/4" dowel and a 3/4" drill bit. The dowel needs to be snug in the 1 x 2's so it stays in place, yet is still easily adjustable.

And the frame was done!

Onto the fabric.

3. (2 minutes)

Many fabric comes in a 44/45" width, so the sides don't need to be hemmed (if you want to hem them you can, but I didn't). To start off, I folded over one end of the fabric and sewed.

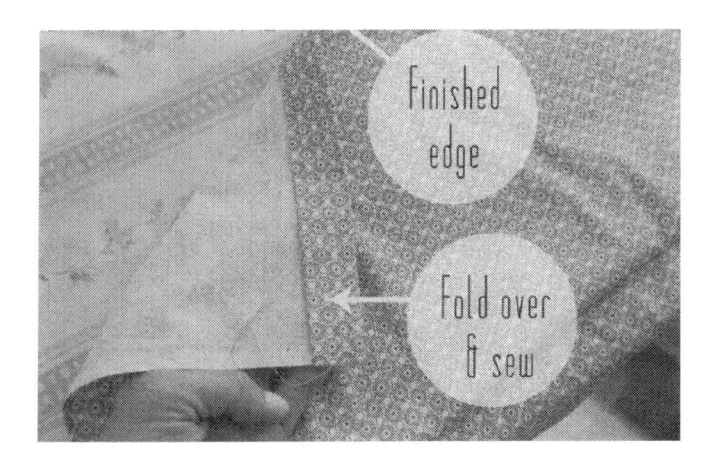

4. (2 minutes)

I draped the fabric (with one finished edge) over the tent frame. I lined up the finished edge side with the bottom of the legs, so I could determine how much needed to be trimmed off the other side – be sure to leave enough fabric to fold over and sew (about 1" extra inch).

Using my Jar O' Ribbons, I picked out 4 fun colors.

5. (2 minutes)

To secure the fabric to the frame, I added ribbon. I cut (4) 12-15" long pieces of ribbon, and sewed the center of it to the right side of each corner using a fun stitch.

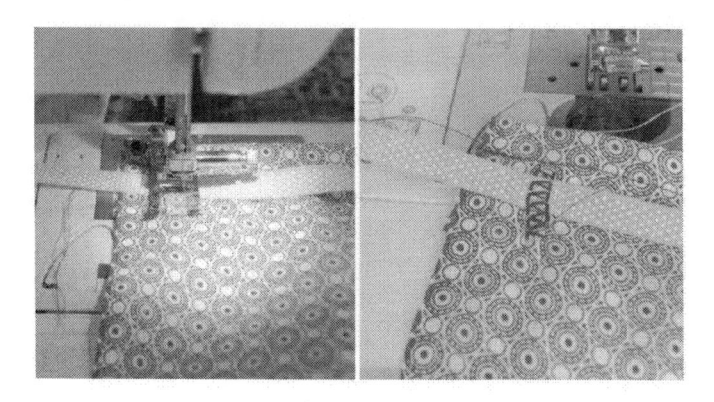

After cutting the loose threads, it was complete!

I draped the fabric over the dowel, attached the 4 ribbons through the 4 bottom holes, and secured. (1 minute)

And the dual play + camping tent was complete.

It's just as easy to disassemble as it is to assemble! Plus it folds right up to store away. I put all the legs together, wrapped the fabric around them, and secured it at both ends with the attached ribbon.

Martial Arts Belt Display

What You'll Need

1/4" plywood (a 2' x 2' piece is plenty)

1 x 2 board

5/8" brad nails

Square

Wood filler

Sandpaper

3/8" elastic

Staple gun and 1/4" staples

Picture hanging hardware

Paint or stain

Saw

I used a table saw to cut down the plywood slats, but you could also use a circular saw.

Don't forget your safety gear when woodworking! Here are my recommendations for safety glasses and ear protection. No excuses!

Instructions

Measure Your Belts

1. Begin by checking the size of your martial arts belts. Fold one up to a size that allows the belt to lay flat in the display without sagging. Mine was 1 3/4" wide and 15" long. The slats of the martial arts belt display need to be a bit wider than the folded belt and a couple inches longer as well.
2. If you happen to have any leftover scraps of wood laying around, they are perfect for this project! I happened to have

some 1/4" plywood that I'd used earlier for my fireplace remodel just sitting around the workshop. If you don't have any leftovers or scraps, head to the store and purchase a 2′ X 2′ plywood panel.

Cut And Sand

1. Use a table saw or circular saw to trim down the plywood into 2" x 18" slats. The back supports are 1 x 2 pieces cut to 17 ½". This is long enough for six belts with 3/4" spacing between them.

2. Sand down any rough edges. Here's a helpful tip: Stack up the slats and sand all the edges at the same time. This also keeps them a consistent size.

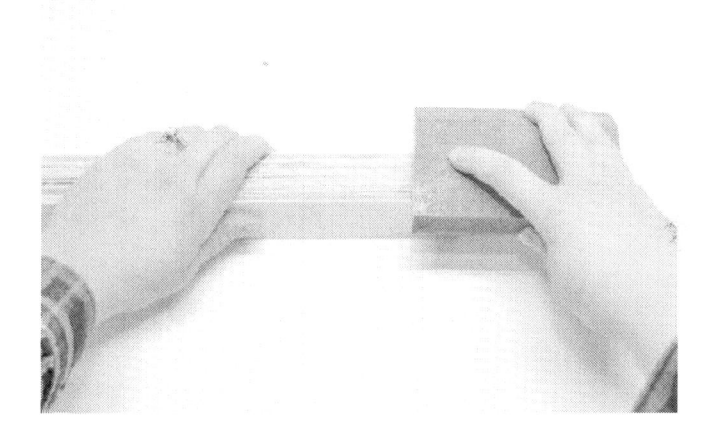

Assemble The Martial Arts Belt Display

1. This martial arts belt display is put together like a ladder, showing the progress from one belt to the next.
2. Lay the first rung of the ladder on top of the 1 x 2 pieces and adjust the spacing until it's ¾" from the bottom and 2" inches in from each side. Use the square to keep the pieces aligned as you clamp it to your work surface.

DIY Woodworking Projects

3. Nail the slats into place with 5/8" brad nails. The Ryobi Airstrike is one of my favorite tools because it's battery operated and doesn't need an air compressor. You can also use a staple gun like this one that also shoots brad nails.

4. A scrap piece of 1 x 2 is the perfect spacer and makes the rest of the process quick and easy. Lay it across the display and butt the next rung up against it. Nail the next one into place, and move the spacer up to the next rung.

5. There should be 3/4" left at the top of the back supports when you're finished attaching all the slats.

Fill Nail Holes And Paint

1. Hide the nail holes with wood filler, then sand down the excess

when dry.
2. Spray paint is the easiest way to tackle these thin pieces. I set up my pop up spray shelter with a lazy susan to rotate the piece as I painted.

Attach Elastic

1. I used 3/8" elastic to hold the belts to the display rack. This makes it simple to add belts as you earn them!
2. Simply staple one end of the elastic to the back of the slat just inside the 1 x 2 supports. Poke the other end through the gap in the slats to the front.

elastic stapled to back of DIY martial arts belt display

3. Hold one of the folded martial arts belts to the front of the slat, and wrap the elastic piece over the top. It's important to have the elastic tight enough to secure the belt without drooping, while not so tight that it makes an indentation.

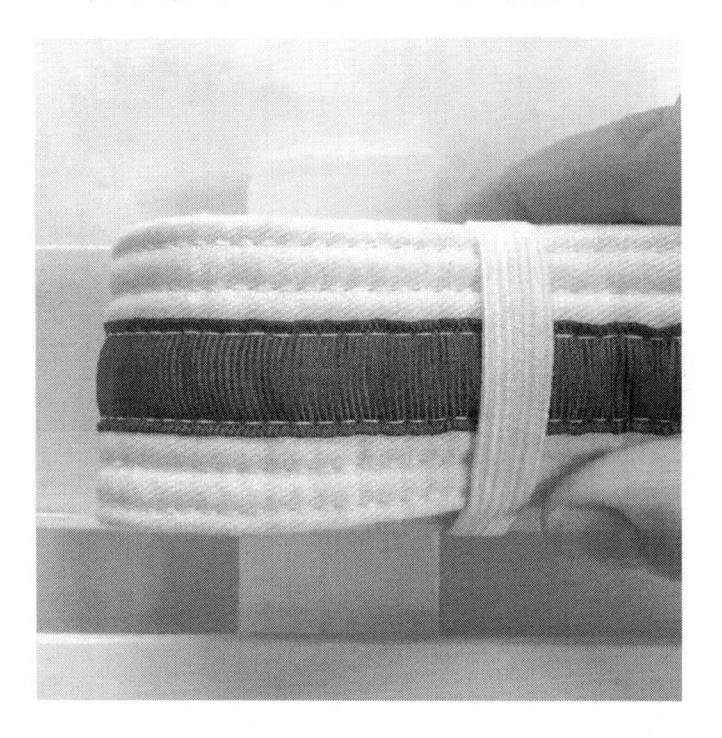

4. Poke the remaining end through the slats to the back again, and mark where you will attach the staples. Measure the

length of the elastic and cut enough pieces for two elastic bands over each belt. Staple them all in place to form loops.

Attach Hanging Hardware

1. Turn the martial arts belt rack over and secure picture hanging hardware to the back. I used eye hooks and wire, but you could use sawtooth hangers as well.

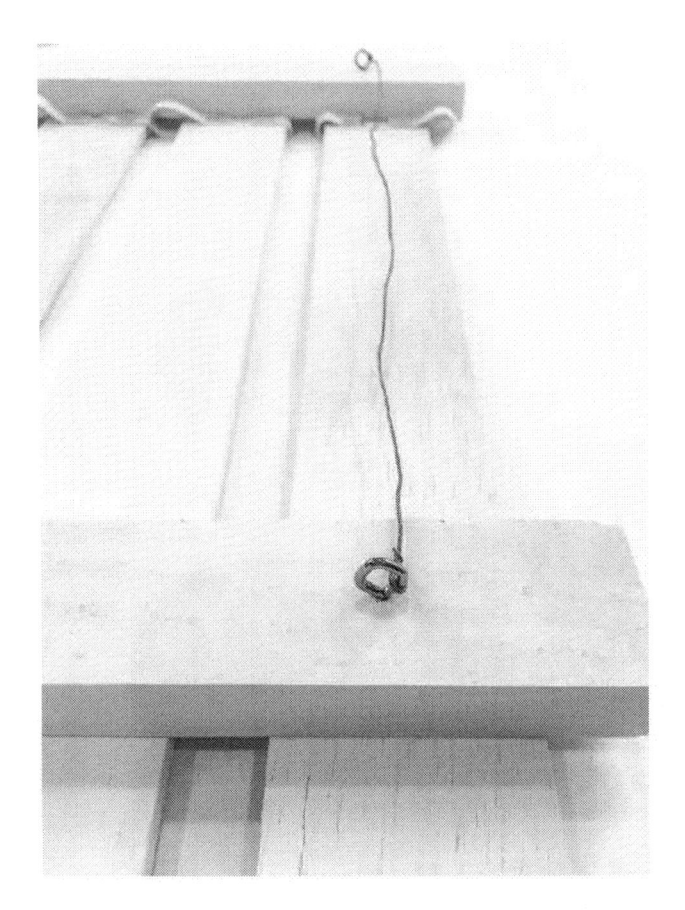

2. Stick each belt under the elastic loops in order they were earned. Then proudly hang your new martial arts belt display on the wall!

Dress-Up Clothes Storage

DIY Woodworking Projects

What You'll Need

As a point of reference, our stage is 48″ x 57″. The list below is for a stage that size. You can easily modify our dimensions to fit your own needs.

For the Actual Stage:

Three pieces of 2″ x 6″ x 10′ Lumber

One Sheet of Sanded 3/4″ Plywood

One - 1″ x 10″ x 8′

3″ Construction Screws

Drill

Circular Saw

Miter Saw (optional, we used this to cut down our 2″ x 6″ pieces, but you could use your circular saw for it.)

Finish Nails and Hammer or Nail Gun

Paint - we opted for Behr Alkyd paint, it works like an oil-based paint in terms of durability, but goes on like latex.

For the Stage Header / Sign:

One - 1″ x 10″ x 8′

Corner Braces

Drill

Wooden Stars

Gold Glitter

Wood Plaque

Hot Glue Gun

Paint – we used the same Behr Allkyd as noted above.

Paint for the Wood Plaque – I used Rustoleum's Sun Yellow Spray Paint.

Vinyl Lettering for the Plaque – I had my friend cut this out for me with her Cricut. You could also use letter stickers that you could find at just about any craft store.

For the Hidden Dress-Up Storage and Curtains:

1 Adjustable Shower Curtain Rod

2 Tension Curtain Rods

4 Curtain Panels – we used these.

Side note: you could totally build this with 2x4s instead of 2x6s. We wanted her stage elevated more than 2x4s would give us though, thus why we went with 2x6s.

Instructions

To Make The Playroom Stage:

1. Cut your 2″ x 6″ pieces to size using a circular saw or miter saw. You'll need the following lengths:

2 cut at 48″

5 cut at 54″ (You will have to sister two pieces of 2″ x 6″ together to get one of these.)

Assemble the pieces as shown below:

DIY Woodworking Projects

2. Attach the outside pieces together first by screwing two 3" construction screws in at all the corners.

3. Attach the inside pieces by screwing two 3" constructions screws in along the outside pieces thru to the inside pieces. Use screws to also sister the two separate 2" x 6" pieces

53

together.
4. Lay the frame on top of the sheet of plywood and trace around it onto the plywood.

5. Use a circular saw to cut along the traced line.
6. Use more construction screws along the corners and edges to attach the plywood to the frame.
7. Paint it!

8. Like I said above, we used Behr's Alkyd paint. I knew this thing would take a beating from the Circus and had actually planned on using oil-based paint which is super durable. However, the paint guy talked me into trying the Alkyd paint since it acts like

oil-based paint in terms of durability but goes on like latex. It does have a smell though. It's not as smelly as oil-based, but enough that I didn't let the Circus sleep in her room for a couple of nights while this thing was still curing. She chose the purple paint color which is called Just a Fairytale. We did two coats of the paint.

9. Cut the 1" x 10" x 8' down to the length of your stage front. You will also have to cut down the height of this piece as well to match the height of your stage so that you don't have a lip on the front of your stage which equals hurt kiddos. With the dimensions of our stage, we cut the 1" x 10" x 8' down to 57" long and 8" tall. Paint this piece as well and then attach it to the front of the stage with finish nails and a hammer or a nail gun. We also added glittered wood stars to ours, which we just attached with hot glue.

That's it for the actual stage part!

To Make The Stage Header / Sign:

1. Cut your 1" x 10" x 8' down to the width of your stage or the width from wall to wall if you are making your stage like ours.
2. Paint and embellish it. We added wooden stars coated with gold glitter, and the sign that reads Landry's Lounge. We hot-glued the stars on and then once the header was hung, I attached the Landry's Lounge sign with a nail gun.

3. Use corner braces to attach the sides of the board to the wall on each edge. If you aren't going wall to wall, you can attach the braces on the board and then onto the ceiling above.

To Create The Hidden Dress-Up Storage And Curtains:

1. Install the shower curtain tension rod toward the back of the stage at a height your child can easily reach.

2. Run one of the tension rods through two of the curtain panels. Hang that curtain tension rod higher up on the wall, almost to the ceiling and slightly in front of the shower curtain tension rod. This will allow the curtains to cover up the play clothes when they are closed. It also creates a pretty backdrop as well.

3. For the curtains in the front of the stage, run two panels through a tension rod, then install it just behind the stage

header.

4. We opted for the yellow curtains (more colors also available!) because they complimented the purple so well. Now, these aren't something I would hang up to block out light because they are thin, but for this little budding performer and her stage, they are perfect.

Printed in Great Britain
by Amazon